What Is A Family?

What Is A Family?

Gretchen Super
Illustrated by Kees de Kiefte

TWENTY-FIRST CENTURY BOOKS
FREDERICK, MARYLAND

To my family—the place where I belong

GS

For Daphne, Caspar, and Oskar

KDK

Library of Congress Cataloging in Publication Data

Super, Gretchen
What Is A Family?
Illustrated by Kees de Kiefte

Includes index.
Summary: Examines the concept of family, the different kinds of families found in society, and the interpersonal relationships that make them function.
1. Family—Juvenile literature. [1. Family. 2. Family life.]
I. Kiefte, Kees de, ill. II. Title. III. Series: Your Family Album.
HQ518.S84   1991   306.85—dc20   90-24380   CIP   AC
ISBN 0-941477-63-0

Published by

Twenty-First Century Books
38 South Market Street
Frederick, Maryland 21701

Text Copyright © 1991
Twenty-First Century Books

Illustrations Copyright © 1991
Kees de Kiefte

Printed in the United States of America

10 9 8 7 6 5 4 3 2 1

Table of Contents

Chapter 1: What Is A Family?

7

Chapter 2: A Family Goes Round And Round

16

Chapter 3: A Family Is About Sharing

28

Chapter 4: Conflict In A Family

41

Chapter 5: Living In A Family

49

Words You Need To Know

54

Index

56

What Is A Family?

What is a family?

Does that sound like a silly question?
Everyone knows what a family is.
A family is who you live with.

But there are many different
kinds of families.

Look at Rachel's family.
Rachel lives with her mom and dad
and her brother, Jake.
Soon there will be a new baby
in her family.
And she lives with two cats,
three gerbils, and one goldfish.
They are a family.

Here is José's family.
He lives with his mom and dad
and baby brother.
José's grandmother and Uncle Ricky
live with him, too.
They are a family.

Look at Peter's family.

He lives with his mother and father.

They adopted Peter when he was
just a baby.

He has a pet poodle named Freddy.

They are a family.

Carly lives with her mom.
Her big sister, Marie, is away at college.
So Carly takes good care of Marie's
cat, Puffin.
Carly loves it when Marie comes home
for the weekend.
They are a family.

Tasha has two families.
Her mother and father are divorced.
Tasha lives with her father, stepmother,
and stepbrother during the week.
They are a family.

And she lives
with her mother
on weekends.
They are a family,
too.

Eric's mom and dad are not able to
take care of him right now.
He is living with his foster parents.
They have two children of their own.
But Eric's parents visit him often.
For now, Eric has two families, too.

Who are the people in your family?
Who are your brothers and sisters?
Who are your grandparents?
Who are your aunts and uncles
and cousins?
Can you list all the people
in your family?

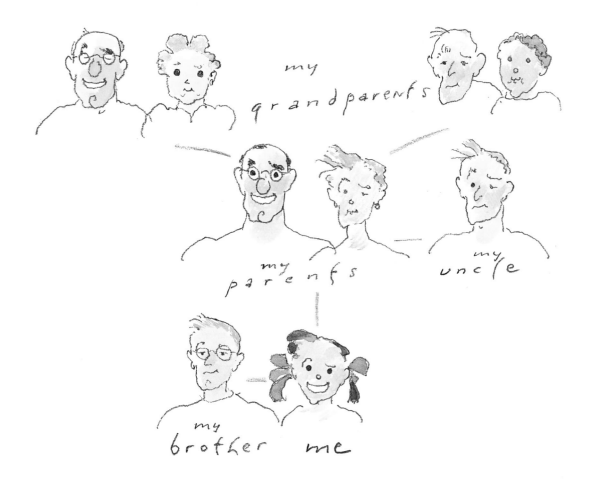

Every family is different.
Every family is a different group
of people.

But a family is more than a group
of people.
A family is more than mothers
and fathers.
It is more than brothers and sisters.
A family is more than aunts
and uncles and cousins.

What is a family?

A family is a group of people who
take care of each other.
They are people who share
their lives together.
A family shares good times.
A family shares hard times.

Every family is different.
And every family is the same, too.
Your family is the place
where you belong.

2

A Family Goes Round And Round

Where is the beginning of a family?
It is hard to say where a family begins.

You might say that a family
is like a circle.
Where is the beginning
of a circle?
A circle goes round
and round.
It has no beginning.
It has no end.

A family goes round and round, too.
It goes through many changes.
But you are always part of a family.

A family starts with two people
who love each other.
They are two people who want to
take care of each other.
They want to share their lives together.

They may decide to get married.
They want to become husband and wife.

When two people become husband
and wife, it is a time to celebrate.
It is a time to celebrate the start
of a new family.

It is a time to make promises.
When two people get married, they
promise to share their lives together.

It is a time to make plans.
When two people get married, they
begin a new life together.
There are many decisions to make.
One of the most important decisions
is about children.

Do you ever pretend that you are
grown-up?
Maybe you pretend that you are a
mother or a father.
It's fun to play that you have a baby.

But having a real baby is a big job.
Now there is a new person
to take care of.
There is a new person to love.

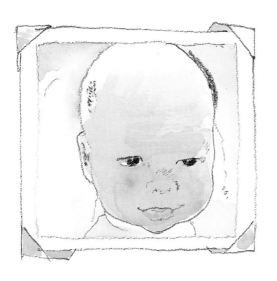 

Don't newborn babies look so tiny?
They can't do anything for themselves.
They need someone to take care
of them all of the time.

But babies grow up very quickly.
Soon they are as old as you.
They have learned how to do
many new things.
And, like you, they are learning how
to take care of themselves.

One day, they will be grown-up and
ready to live on their own.
They are ready to take care of themselves.
They may decide to start a new family.
They may even decide to have their
own children.

Then the mother and father will be
a grandmother and grandfather.
There will be grandchildren to love
and take care of.

The family keeps growing and changing.

And, every day, the grandchildren will
learn new things.
And, one day, they will be grown-up.
Then they will be able to take care
of themselves.
They may decide to start
a new family, too.

A family is like a circle.
It has no beginning.
It has no end.

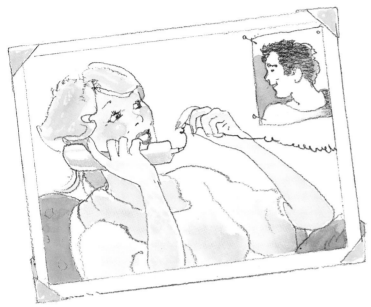

A family goes round and round.
It goes through many changes.
But you are always part of a family.

3

A Family Is About Sharing

A family is about sharing.

A family shares good times.
Good times can happen anywhere.
They can happen anytime.

Good times happen when a family
works together.

Tasha helps her dad and stepmother
get dinner ready.
She makes the salad and sets the table.
Sometimes she plans the whole meal.
Her favorite dinner is pancakes
with applesauce.
"Not again!" her stepbrother laughs.

Eric likes to help his foster father
do the laundry.
They go to the laundromat together.
Eric is in charge of putting the coins
in the washer and dryer.
One time, his foster father put too
much soap in the washer.
What a mess there was that day!

Good times happen when a family
plays together.

Peter's family likes to play
cards together.
Peter shuffles the deck and deals
the cards.
He has fun when he wins.
"But I even have fun when I lose,"
Peter laughs.

Carly and her mom like
to exercise together.
They put on a fun workout tape.
Carly says her mom grunts and
groans a lot.
"Let's turn the music up real loud,"
Carly says.
"It's loud enough," her mother grunts
and groans.

Good times happen when a family
shares special times.

Every Sunday morning, Rachel's dad
takes Rachel and Jake to breakfast.
Rachel always has scrambled eggs,
potatoes, toast, and juice.
"Why don't you try something new?"
her father asks.
"I like this fine," Rachel answers.

José's family has a quiet time
before dinner.
His grandmother says a special prayer
in Spanish.
José doesn't understand all
of the words.
But he knows what they mean.
He knows his family is thankful for
the many good things they have.

A family shares hard times, too.

Tasha misses her mom
during the week.
But she knows she can always
call her at work.
No matter how busy Tasha's mom is,
she makes time to talk.
"How's my girl?" she asks.
It makes Tasha feel better just
to hear her mom's voice.

José remembers when he started
first grade.
It was a big day for him.
He was too nervous to eat the special
breakfast that Grandma made.

Uncle Ricky walked José to the bus stop.
He stayed with José until the bus came.
"Hey, you're going to be okay," Uncle
Ricky promised.

Rachel is happy about the new baby—
at least she is most of the time.
But she can remember what it was like
when Jake was born.
He cried all of the time.
Her mom and dad were always tired.
It seemed like no one had any time
for her.
"Will it be the same way this time?"
Rachel worries.

Carly remembers when Marie got sick.
She went to visit Marie in the hospital.
One night, Carly saw that her mother
had been crying.
Carly put her arms around her mother.
"It will be all right," Carly whispered.

Peter's dad lost his job last year.
It was a very hard time for the family.
Peter's mom and dad made a plan
to save money.
Peter said he could save money, too.
He decided not to buy ice cream
from the ice cream man.
His dad and mom were very proud
of him.

A family is about sharing.

A family shares good times.

A family shares hard times.

What times does your family share?

Conflict In A Family

Sometimes it is hard to share in a family.
The people in a family may like
different things.
They may not agree with each other.
They may argue about these differences.
When people don't agree about their
differences, there is conflict.

Rachel and Jake always argue
about watching television.
They never want to watch
the same show.
One day, Rachel's mom got tired
of their fighting.
She didn't let them watch anything
for two weeks!

José's family is always arguing
about the toothpaste tube.
"Who is squeezing the tube from the
top again?" José's father wants to know.
"I wonder who that could be," José says.

Conflict in a family can be about
everyday things.
But conflict in a family can also be
more serious.

Carly remembers when her mom
would not let Marie go to the beach.
Marie was so angry that she hardly
spoke to their mom.
It was quiet in the house for days.

Sometimes conflict is not so quiet.
Peter knows when his mom and dad
are arguing about money.
Their voices get loud and angry.

Most times a family finds a way
to solve its conflicts.
They work things out on their own.
Rachel watches one of Jake's shows,
and Jake watches one of hers.
"I guess you were right about the
beach, Mom," Marie finally said.
"But what about next year?"
Together, Peter's parents make a plan
to save money.

And José tries to remember to squeeze
the toothpaste tube from the bottom.

Other times a family needs help
to solve its conflicts.
Rachel's mom and dad used to argue
all the time.
It seemed that they were always angry.

Her parents went to talk
with a marriage counselor.
The counselor showed them new ways
to talk about their problems.
"We used to just talk to each other,"
Rachel's dad told her. "Now we
listen to each other."

There was so much conflict in Eric's family that his parents were not even able to take care of him.

Eric went to live with a foster family. Now Eric and his parents go together to a family counselor.

They are working hard to solve their problems so Eric can come home soon.

Sometimes, even with help, a family can't solve its problems.

The people in the family are not able to share their lives together.

The family has to change.

Tasha remembers when her parents decided to end their marriage.

They couldn't get along, and they didn't want to live together anymore.

One night, they told Tasha they were getting a divorce.

"What's going to happen to me?"
Tasha cried.
Tasha and her parents talked about
many things that night.

"We will always love you," her
mother said.
"And we will always be your family,"
her father added.

Conflict can make people feel sad
or angry.
It can make people feel lonely
or scared.

But conflict is a normal part of living
in a family.
There are differences in every family,
and people disagree at times.
When people love each other, they try
to solve their conflicts.

Working together to solve a conflict
can even help a family.
It can help people listen to each other.
It can help people learn about
their differences.
It can help people accept each other.
Working together to solve a conflict
can make a family strong.

Living In A Family

Imagine that you do not have a family.

No dad or mom.

No brothers or sisters.

No aunts or uncles or cousins.

Imagine that it is just you.

What would it be like?

Do you think it would be fun?

You could eat candy for breakfast.
You could eat ice cream for dinner.
But who would take care of you?

You wouldn't have to clean your room.
You wouldn't have to take a bath.
But who would you talk to?
Who would you play with?

You could watch as much television
as you want.
You could stay up as late as you like.

But who would listen to you
when you felt happy?
Who would be there for you
when you felt sad?

You need a family.
You need a family to take care of you.
A family is a group of people who
take care of each other.
They are people who share
what they have.

But they are people who share
more than things.
A family shares time.
They work and play together.
They share special times.
They share good times and hard times.

And they are people who share
more than time.
A family shares feelings.
They share plans and dreams.
They share hopes and memories.
Most of all, a family shares love.

What is a family?

Every family is different.
And every family is the same, too.

Everyone knows what a family is.
Your family is the place
where you belong.

Words You Need To Know

There are many different kinds of families. "Your Family Album" will help you understand what a family is and what different families are like. Here are some words you should know:

adoption agency: a service that helps families adopt children

adoptive family: when parents have a child they did not give birth to

birth-parents: the man and woman who give birth to a child

blended family: when people live together who used to live in other families

conflict: when people in a family don't agree about their differences

divorce: when a husband and wife decide to end their marriage

extended family: when different relatives live together in a family

family: a group of people who care about each other and share their lives together

family counselor: a person who helps a family solve conflict

foster family: when a new set of parents takes care of a child for a while

husband: a man who is married

marriage: when a man and a woman decide to become husband and wife

marriage counselor: a person who helps a husband and wife solve conflict

nuclear family: when a mother, father, and their children live together in a family

single-parent family: when only one parent lives with a family

stepfamily: another word for a blended family

wife: a woman who is married

Index

adopted 9

baby 7-9, 20-22, 37

children 12, 19, 23

conflict 41-48

differences 41, 48

divorce 11, 46

family counselor 46

foster family 30, 46

foster father 30

foster parent 12

good times 14, 28-34, 40, 52

grandchildren 24-25

grandfather 24

grandmother 8, 24, 34, 36

grandparents 13

hard times 14, 35-40, 52

husband 17-18

marriage 17, 19, 46

marriage counselor 45

parent 12, 44-47

sharing 14, 17-19, 28, 33, 35, 40-41, 46, 52

stepbrother 11, 28

stepmother 11, 28

wife 17-18